have you wondered how wondered how computers draw webpages?

MW00884382

they use a special language called HTML, which means

Hyper

TEXT

MARKUP

language

HTML is made of building blocks, called tags!

<body>

<img>

<input>

</body>

tags
start with "<"
and
end with ">"

body img

h1

p

br

in the middle of "<" and ">", you can choose from a list of special words.

Like a magic spell, it will make something appear!

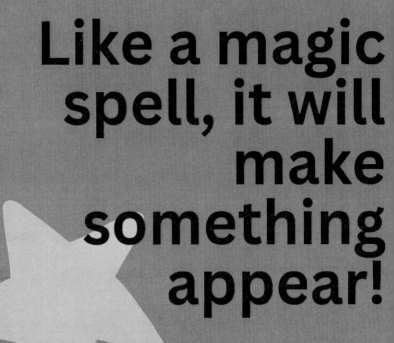

Check out some examples!

\<img\>

this is short for image!

\<button>

Click Me!

This makes a button that you can click!

<dialog>

This is an open dialog window

This makes a box pop up!

<ul>

- Cat
- Dog
- Sheep

This makes a list with bullet points!

1. Cat
2. Dog
3. Sheep

This makes a list with numbers!

tags usually come in pairs like twins!

<body>
</body>

<p>
</p>

Adding "/" makes a tag an ending tag

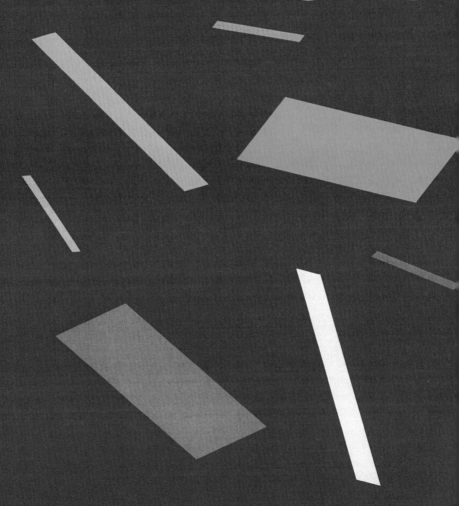

the first tag
tells you when
an element
starts

START

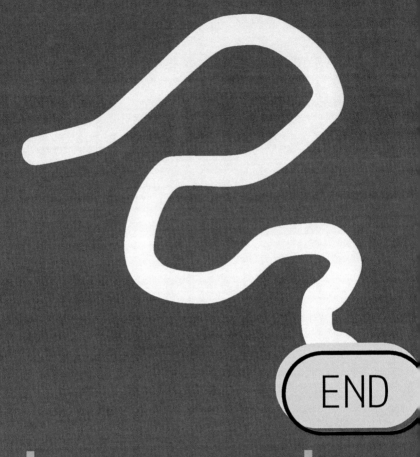

END

the second tag tells you when an element ends

you can put elements in other elements!

```
<p> <- start of a paragraph
   You are smart!
   <b> YAY! </b> <- bold text
   Great job!
</p> <- end paragraph
```

this is called nesting.

the element on the inside is called the child.

the element on the **outside** is **called the parent.**

it's like when someone gives you a hug!

their arms are wrapped around you like the parent element around the child element!

in the next book, we'll learn how to style elements with CSS!

congrats!

you're ready to be a web developer!

check out our other books!

baby's first CSS
baby's first JS
word games

Made in United States
North Haven, CT
27 September 2024

58018923R00015